American Archaeology

UNCOVERS
THE UNDERGROUND
RAILROAD

LOIS MINER HUEY

Marshall Cavendish
Benchmark
New York

ACKNOWLEDGMENTS

Series Designer: Kay Petronio

Consultant: James A. Delle,
Chair, Department of Anthropology and Sociology,
Kutztown University of Pennsylvania

Marshall Cavendish • 99 White Plains Road • Tarrytown, New York 10591
www.marshallcavendish.us

Library of Congress Cataloging–in–Publication Data
Huey, Lois Miner.
American archaeology uncovers the Underground Railroad / by Lois Miner Huey.
p. cm. — (American archaeology)
Includes bibliographical references and index.
ISBN 978–0–7614–4267–7
1. Underground Railroad—Juvenile literature. 2. Fugitive slaves—United States—History—
19th century—Juvenile literature. 3. Antislavery movements—United States—History—
19th century—Juvenile literature. 4. Archaeology and history—United States—Juvenile literature.
5. Excavations—Archaeology—United States—Juvenile literature. I. Title.
E450.H874 2010
973.7'115—dc22
2009003168

Photo research by : Tracey Engel

Cover photo, *top*, Students conduct a dig at a science camp sponsored by the University of Connecticut. Artifacts at
bottom, *left*, St. Christopher medal found at Fort Mose, Florida; *center*, ceramic cup from the Parker House, Ripley,
Ohio; *right*, cast iron angel from the Parker House.
Cover photo: AP Images/Bob Child (top); Stephen McBride (bottom, left);
Lisa Haitz (bottom, middle; bottom, right); iStock © Vishnu Mulakala,
back cover; iStock © Alex Nikado
Title page: iStock © Lisa Thorinberg, iStock © Vishnu Mulakala

The photographs in this book are used by permission and through the courtesy of: Alamy: Jim West, 46–47. AP
Images: Bob Child, 4. Doug Armstrong: 22, 24, 27. Art Resource: Smithsonian American Art Museum, Washington,
DC, 9. Camp Nelson Civil War Heritage Park: 42. Corbis: Bettmann, 20–21. Courtesy of the Florida Museum of
Natural History–Historical Archaeology Collections: 17, 18 (both), 19. Florida National Guard Heritage Art Collection –
Department of Military Affairs – State of Florida: 15. Karolyn Smardz Frost: 48, 50, 52. Getty Images: Hulton Archive,
12–13, 40–41; Mike Simons, 54–55. Lisa Haitz: 34–35, 36, 37 (both), 38. Institute for Canine Forensics/Adela Morris:
44. Library of Congress, Prints and Photographs Division: 10, 26, 31 (both). Courtesy of Catherine Lott–Divis: 28–29,
30. Stephen McBride: 43. Printed with permission of the New York State Museum, Albany, NY, 12230: 5 (bottom).
Courtesy of Chris Ricciardi–Alyssa Loorya: 33 (both).
3; iStock © Eric Isselee, iStock © Kals Tomats, 4; iStock © ObservePhoto, 5; Shutterstock © Najin, 6; iStock © Richard
Goerg, iStock © Richard Cano, 7; iStock © Alex Nikado, 10; iStock © Emrah Oztas, iStock © Torsten Lorenz, 14;
Shutterstock © Biuliq, 44; iStock © Norman Chan

Printed in: Malaysia
135642

CONTENTS

WHAT IS Historical Archaeology?

Archaeologists dig into the ground to find food bones, building remains, and tools used by people in the past. Historical archaeologists are looking for clues about what happened in America after Europeans arrived.

A group of students at the "Kids Are Scientists, Too" camp conduct an archaeological investigation at the former site of an eighteenth–century home on the University of Connecticut campus at Storrs.

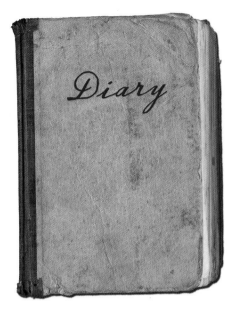

Yes, written documents tell some of the story. Historical archaeologists research documents like maps, diaries, land deeds, and letters to help understand what happened on a site. But those documents do not usually talk about regular people, the ones who did not write letters or diaries. Historical archaeologists are especially interested in learning about the lives of servants, poor farmers, and soldiers who built America.

How do archaeologists do this? By studying people's garbage.

What folks used and threw away tells more about their daily lives than objects kept on shelves out of harm's way. Archaeologists want to study the stuff that did not make it into museums—objects that were broken and discarded after much use. The garbage.

Broken dishes and glassware tell archaeologists what people of the past chose for setting their tables. Studying the bones of people's food, as well as their butchering techniques, provides information about what people ate and how they cooked. When archaeologists measure uncovered house and barn foundations, they find out how people crafted buildings, what size and shape they were, and how they were used. Buttons, straight pins, gun parts, and toys are clues to how people dressed, defended their homes, and spent their leisure time.

How do historical archaeologists know they are collecting information about people who lived in the 1600s rather than people from the 1800s? They use a method called stratigraphy (struh-TIG-ra-fee). Over time, layers of soil called strata build up on a site through natural causes or when people add their own materials. By carefully scraping away the soil with small tools, archaeologists dig down through time. They begin with upper levels of soil, in which they may find nineteenth-century layers. As they work their way down, they reach eighteenth-century layers, seventeenth-century layers, and so on. In some areas, the layers go back as far as Viking times. Prehistoric Native-American layers are often found at the deepest level. The scientists dig each layer separately and collect its artifacts. Once the uppermost layer has been removed, the archaeologists have dug through the lives of everyone who lived on that site at a given time.

Based on what they find, archaeologists interpret the artifacts from each time period to understand how people's lives changed. *Change* is a big word in archaeology. How people lived—and how and when that changed— is an important part of the interpretation. As new evidence appears, archaeologists sometimes have to change their interpretations. That makes archaeology really interesting.

Stratigraphy is the key to understanding the past. Sticking a shovel straight down into the ground and pulling up the soil would disturb the stratigraphy, mix up the layers, and mix up the time periods. Archaeologists use shovel testing only to find a site. Then they switch over to small tools and painstakingly remove the layers one by one.

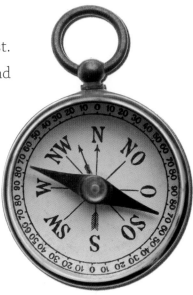

As archaeologists study a site, they carefully draw, map, and photograph building remains. Artifacts are taken back to the lab, where workers wash and store them. Codes are written on each object so that it is clear exactly where the artifact was found. Scientists run tests on charcoal, soil, and remains found inside bottles. Then the archaeologist writes up the results of the research so everyone can know what was learned. Museum displays often follow.

The world that we think of as ours was thought by people in the past to be theirs. Our knowledge of everyday events in the lives of people who lived long ago seems to be washed away by time. By digging in the ground and studying documents, an archaeologist seems to take a voyage to the distant past in a time machine.

Read about archaeology in books and magazines, go to museums, watch programs on television, and maybe visit a local archaeology dig. Someday you, too, might decide to use the tools of archaeology to study the past.

The Underground Railroad

The Underground Railroad was not under the ground, and it was not a railroad. So how did it get this name?

The word *underground* here means "secret." *Railroad* refers to the way escaped slaves traveled to safety. Because it was so secret, archaeologists have a hard time finding evidence of this "railroad." It was not meant to be found!

A painting done about 1940 by James Michael Newell depicts fugitive slaves being shown a place to hide. The image was painted on a wall of the post office in Dolgeville, New York.

African-American slaves escaped by any means possible. They walked for miles and miles, slept in woods and people's cellars, to reach a place where slavery was not legal. Both black and white people, called conductors, assisted the escaped slaves. Conductors transported some escapees hidden in wagons. Many more Underground Railroad "passengers" traveled by boat or on an actual train.

In the years before 1850, once refugee slaves reached the northern states, they were fairly safe. At the time, the Underground Railroad operated more openly. Conductors were known by their real names, and newspapers published stories about their activities. In 1850, however, the Fugitive Slave Law was passed. This law required every citizen to return fugitive slaves to their owners. Then the Underground Railroad truly became a secretive process—it

Harriet Tubman

The most famous conductor on the Underground Railroad was a slave from Maryland named Harriet Tubman. She escaped in 1849 and made her way to Philadelphia, Pennsylvania. Liberty meant so much to her that she made thirteen dangerous trips south to bring out slaves. This earned Tubman the nickname Moses. Slave owners offered an award for her capture, but she was never caught.

During the Civil War, Tubman returned to the South and worked as a nurse, cook, scout, and spy for the Union army. After the war, Tubman lived in Auburn, New York, in a house given to her, perhaps in honor of her work. Here she lived until her death in 1913. Tubman devoted herself to establishing and running a home for elderly African Americans.

In recent years, archaeologists from Syracuse University excavated areas around Tubman's house as well as the Tubman Home for the Aged. They discovered that the brick house now standing was built after a fire destroyed the original wood house in the 1880s. A large number of Tubman's personal possessions removed during the fire had been redeposited as fill in trenches dug to build the new house. The archaeologists also excavated a kiln used to manufacture the bricks for the house that is now open to visitors.

Elderly Harriet Tubman sitting in a chair, probably at her Auburn, New York home. She lived to be over ninety years old.

went underground—as conductors worked to get the refugees safely to Canada where they would be free.

One source says that by 1800, 1.5 million slaves had been brought to North America from Africa. That does not count the number of African slaves who arrived during the seventeenth century or who were born in North America. No one knows for sure how many slaves escaped to freedom over the many years the Underground Railroad operated. But one conductor, the minister of a church in Syracuse, New York, wrote that he "passed as many as thirty slaves through my hands in a month." This was but one stop on the Underground Railroad and one conductor. Thousands more brave, determined slaves made their escape over the years. They did not know where they were going, where they would end up, or what their future would be. They arrived starved, scared, exhausted, and wearing worn-out clothes. Many were captured and returned to their owners. The bravery of the escapees—and the bravery of people willing to feed, clothe, and send them to the next "station"—is a dramatic story in American history.

One
An Early Underground Railroad

Slaves began to escape from their masters as soon as they arrived from Africa. Almost unknown is the story of a very early Underground Railroad. On this railroad, the refugees went south instead of north!

An engraving from 1754 shows a slave ship arriving in 1619 in Jamestown, Virginia with slaves for sale. This is believed to be the date when commercial slavery began in the English colonies.

The Spanish owned Florida until 1763, when they gave it to the British as part of a peace agreement called the Treaty of Paris. During Spanish rule, slaves who made it across the border to Florida were given their freedom as long as they agreed to become Roman Catholic and to help defend Spain from her enemies. So an Underground Railroad operated in southern states, especially the Carolinas and Georgia, from 1687 until the 1760s. The conductors often were American Indians who helped shepherd the refugees to Florida. In 1719, officials from South Carolina wrote that the Spanish were making pitch and tar with the help of black slaves stolen "by their Indians from our frontier settlements."

Documents show that the first arrivals were twelve exhausted Africans: eight men, three women, and a three-year-old child. They came in 1687 by boat, perhaps a canoe, through swamps and rivers. Many more followed, and by 1738, the now-free slaves had moved a few miles north of the city of St. Augustine. They formed their own community called Fort Mose, (Moh-say)

A painting by Jackson Walker in the 1990s shows the 1740 battle between the English and Spanish at Fort Mose with the former slaves assisting the Spanish.

which had been established by the Spanish governors of Florida. Here, they farmed, hunted, fished, and received food from the Spanish in return for helping to protect Florida from outside invasions.

When British troops attacked in 1740, the inhabitants moved back to St. Augustine, but some joined a surprise counterattack on the British and drove them away from Fort Mose. The fort was destroyed during this fierce battle, so the former slaves stayed in St. Augustine for another twelve years.

In 1752 a new Fort Mose and town were rebuilt at a nearby site, occupied eventually by twenty-two households and sixty-seven residents, including fifteen children. When the British gained Florida, the inhabitants of the fort and town refused to live under British slave laws. They packed up their belongings and moved to Cuba, where they were safe under Spanish law. The second Fort Mose and town disappeared by 1812.

Slave Resistance

A Spanish explorer established a town in Georgia in 1526. One hundred African slaves were among the six hundred settlers. Illness, trouble with American Indians, and a slave rebellion caused the colony to fail within two months. The colonists left, but many of the slaves escaped and lived in freedom with the Indians.

Slaves rebelled in South Carolina several times during the eighteenth century. In 1739, after hearing about a Spanish settlement called Fort Mose, slaves near Charleston, South Carolina, rose up and began marching to Florida. The white militia discovered them and crushed the revolt.

Recent archaeological work in Florida and in the Dismal Swamp of Virginia and North Carolina has uncovered remains of more settlements by fugitive slaves who escaped from slavery but never left the area. Instead, they went deep into swamps and other unwanted land to establish hidden communities.

Finding the forts

In 1994, Florida archaeologists decided to search for the two forts. They found the first Fort Mose by using thermal imagery provided by NASA. Disturbed soils produce heat differently from natural soil. Thermal imaging locates sites by the heat that shows up on special cameras. The first Fort Mose is now underwater and is not very accessible for excavations.

Using satellite imagery also supplied by NASA, along with map studies and core drillings into marshy ground, the archaeologists then located the second Fort Mose on what is now a small island. The archaeologists mapped the island and recorded each rise and fall in the landscape. As a result, they easily found the fort's outline, as well as its moat.

Digging and discovering

Excavations over a three-year period revealed a large, three-sided fort with the entryway (the fourth or open side) facing toward the river. The fort walls, each about the length of two-thirds of a football field, were built of earth covered with marsh clay and surrounded by a moat filled with prickly pear cactus. An enemy army would have had a hard time crossing that moat!

Inside the fort there was a watchtower, a church, and some oval houses like those built in Africa. The houses were from 12 to 20 feet (3.7 to 6 meters) in diameter and stood on posts. Documents say they had palm-thatched roofs. Cannons and swivel guns sat on the fort's packed-earth walls.

The archaeologists found that the inhabitants ate simple foods: figs, nuts, squash, melons, beans, oranges, small blue huckleberries, plums, sour persimmons, blueberries, blackberries, grapes, meat, fish, shellfish, turtles, rabbits, and deer. To prepare the food, they used corn-grinding stones, Indian clay cooking pots, and English ceramic pots. Some of the men married Indian women, and each family prepared this food according to its own custom. The settlers also used storage jars, pewter spoons, and wine bottles.

A drawing of Fort Mose as it may have looked in the 1700s. The fort's open side faces the river, and the farming fields are outside the walls on the other three sides. Note the small circular hut much like those built in Africa.

St. Christopher medal found by archaeologists at Fort Mose

Gun parts and military buttons from the soldiers' uniforms were evidence of fort life. Other military objects were gunflints, used to produce the spark to fire guns, and cannonballs. Pins, needles, nonmilitary buttons, buckles, and thimbles suggested that the people wore European-type clothing that they made themselves.

No luxurious items were found, although there were a brass finger ring, a St. Christopher medal, and rosary beads. These religious items, along with the existence of a church and a priest's house, suggest that the refugees did become Catholics, as the Spanish required. However, the blue beads archaeologists found could mean that old beliefs continued anyway. Most of the occupants were from West Africa or descended from West Africans. There, blue beads were believed to prevent illness and evil spirits. Perhaps the refugees who lived at Fort Mose continued to hold such beads—just in case.

Everyday items, such as nails and a flint strike-a-light for making fires, were common, as were white clay tobacco pipes.

Shoe buckles found at Fort Mose

Why is Fort Mose important?

The existence of this very early Underground Railroad challenges the notion that African Americans were passive slaves. Almost from the very beginning of slavery in North America, they tried to escape to freedom. Fort Mose was

A glass bead found at Fort Mose, probably for trade with the Native Americans

the first legal, free black community in what is now the United States. The archaeology has shown what the fort looked like and how the people lived. This gives a richer, more balanced view of the black experience in America. African Americans' determination to be free continued, as many former slaves chose to leave their homes in Florida rather than to continue living under British slavery laws.

Two
Faces Left Behind

Archaeologists have uncovered the mystery of seven faces on clay walls under a church in Syracuse, New York. These images are the work of runaway slaves hiding in the church basement. When the archaeologists found them, the faces were in danger of breaking away from the wall. Could they be saved? *Should* they be saved? Did they date to the time of the Underground Railroad? Or, as some people claimed, were they created in the 1940s as a Halloween party project to scare children in a dark basement? Archaeologists were asked to discover when the faces were created.

A late–nineteenth–century painting by Charles T. Webber shows a family helping a group of fugitive slaves.

The Wesleyan Methodist Church in Syracuse was a well-known stop on the Underground Railroad. Dedicated to the abolition of slavery, the congregation grew to 15,000 people by 1844 and had built its church by 1847. Members actively helped the Underground Railroad and set up rooms inside the church to publish abolitionist newspapers. Syracuse was ideally situated as a stop on the Underground Railroad. The open area north of the city was sparsely settled and led directly to the Canadian border.

Spooky memories

Archaeologists began their work on the mysterious faces by interviewing people familiar with the church. When eighty-three-year-old Laura Grover

One of the faces carved on the clay wall of the Syracuse, New York church. The person depicted seems to be looking to the side, as though watching for slave catchers.

was a child, she and some friends skipped church services and sneaked down to explore the basement. It was dark and spooky; they could not see much. But she clearly remembers running her hands across the faces on the wall. Later on, she was glad she had not known they were really faces—she would have been so scared! This happened in 1923, so archaeologists could conclude that the faces were there prior to the 1940s Halloween party.

Documents and newspapers from the 1800s report that slaves were kept in the church auditorium during daylight, but "sometimes the slaves were hidden beneath the church" at night. The documents also show changes made to the church over the years, and they tell of a furnace fire in 1898.

Before digging in the basement floor, archaeologists photographed and drew each clay face. They mapped the locations of the faces, the current furnace, a tunnel or narrow passageway, and the coal storage areas.

A tricky tunnel

Archaeologists could tell that the narrow tunnel-passageway in the basement of the church was dug by hand, as pick and shovel marks were visible on its walls. Partway into the basement, the tunnel takes a turn. From the outside looking down the tunnel, it appears to end right there. It is only from inside the tunnel that you can see the turn. Wouldn't this trick be useful to keep slaves hidden when people peered into the basement?

After the turn, the tunnel leads into an open area, where the clay faces once clung to the walls. Five were close to the furnace. The coal furnace, which has been turned into a gas furnace, sits at a lower level than the passageway with a wood beam running between the furnace and the passageway. After removing wood debris, excavators revealed a clay bench next to the furnace. The bench is the right size for someone to lie down—it is too big just to be a seat for the furnace man. This raised bench would have kept sleepers off the wet floor and close to the heat.

Excavations in the furnace area uncovered a layer from the 1898 fire layer and, below that, five layers that accumulated before the fire. In these layers was a brick platform that once supported an old wood-burning furnace. The remains showed that both the early furnace and the passageway were built before the 1898 fire. They existed when slaves were hiding in the church basement.

A possible image of Frederick Douglass. The hairstyle and the date under the image suggest it is the famous emancipator.

During the 1898 fire, the two clay faces closest to the furnace were scorched by the heat and flames. This "fired" the clay, which helped preserve just those two. Archaeologists now knew the faces were there before the 1898 fire.

Archaeologists concluded that both the tunnel passageway and the clay faces existed as early as 1850. Archaeological evidence, together with interviews and documentary information, strongly supported the conclusion that the clay faces were made by runaway slaves hiding in the basement of the church.

Why did slaves make these faces?

No one knows for sure why the refugees sculpted the seven faces. The archaeologists were able to lift fingerprints embedded in three of the faces—the fingerprints of the person who was molding the clay. Each set of fingerprints is different, indicating that a different person made each face. The faces have various sizes and shapes, as well as different facial features and hairstyles. This also suggests that a different person created each one.

The seven faces were visible only after the turn in the passageway. Two were on walls on either side of the turn, as though to welcome visitors. The other five faces were close to the old wood furnace. The faces were carved between 4 and 4.5 feet (122 and 137 centimeters) up from the floor. Over time some of the faces cracked, so archaeologists could tell how they were created. The artists first gouged out oval forms in the wall. They then applied wet clay to the surface, building up the faces first before adding features like eyes, a nose, and a mouth. Black ash was used to darken the clay used for the eyes on two of the faces. After years of erosion, only a few facial features remain. The faces appear to have tightly curled hair done in various styles that were popular before the Civil War.

Excavators found candle wax on some of the faces. They guess that the wax came from candles that the artists used as they worked. Another possibility is that later sightseers accidentally dripped candle wax on the faces.

Future face time

After the archaeological work at Wesleyan Methodist, interest and concern for the seven faces grew rapidly. Meanwhile, the church was turned into a restaurant, and after its new furnace was turned on, some of the faces deteriorated even more. The archaeologists attracted the attention of some professional conservators at a national archaeological conference. These experts donated their time to travel to Syracuse and to figure out how to save the faces.

It took four more years, but once enough money was raised, the faces were carefully removed from the basement walls, conserved, and installed in a new exhibit at the Onondaga Historical Association building, located one block away from the church-restaurant. Visitors can see them in this location today.

Face #1: Frederick Douglass

The archaeologists named it Face #1, but that does not mean it was the first one created. Many people have remarked that this well-preserved face, partially burned by the 1898 fire, resembles that of Frederick Douglass. Douglass was a famous black abolitionist who lived nearby. Under this face, someone carved the date 1817—the year of Douglass's birth. It appears this face was carved as a tribute to him.

A photograph of Frederick Douglass taken in January 1850

Frederick Douglass's birth name was Frederick Augustus Washington Bailey. Once he escaped from slavery in 1838, however, he changed his name to put slave catchers off his trail. Arriving in New Bedford, Massachusetts, a well-known whaling city and one of the safest places for runaway slaves, Douglass stayed at the home of Nathan and Polly Johnson. Nathan suggested to Frederick that he take the name Douglas—the hero of a book Nathan was reading at the time (*Lady of the Lake* by Sir Walter Scott). Frederick liked the idea but added an extra *s* to the name.

The Wesleyan Methodist Church in Syracuse, New York, a well-known station on the Underground Railroad and original location of the clay faces

Faces toward freedom

Refugees who hid in the basement of the Wesleyan Methodist Church were far from home, yet they were close to their goal: freedom. The fact that some of them spent time carving representations of either themselves or other people could represent the good feelings they had. Were the faces created by a whole group of people all at once? Did someone create the first one, followed by others who were inspired to make more? We will probably never know. But the faces remain a symbol of how these people felt and how they chose to express their feelings.

Three
Bound for Brooklyn

When archaeologists dig around historic buildings, they often study the building itself, too. After all, it is the largest artifact on the site! When this is done, it is called above-ground archaeology.

This is what happened at the Lott House, located in Brooklyn, New York. Many runaway slaves found shelter in Brooklyn, which is very close to New York City. Brooklyn was an important hub on the Underground Railroad. It had a large waterfront filled with boats that could transport slave refugees.

A photograph taken about 1909 of the Lott House. Courtesy of Catherine Lott–Divis

Brooklyn was also home to a population of free African Americans and many antislavery churches. In 2007, in recognition of Brooklyn's role in helping escaped slaves, the city of New York gave a street in downtown Brooklyn the alternative name of Abolitionist Place.

Was there a lot to dig at the Lott House?

The Hendrick I. Lott House is a Dutch house built before the Revolutionary War. The house originally had one room but expanded gradually to a twenty-two-room manor house. The surrounding farmland gradually was sold off as Brooklyn grew. Archaeologists from Brooklyn College wanted to study how the old house, and the landscape around it, changed over time from a farm to a city house. In the ground, they found that the soil layers had become quite jumbled by all the changes made to the landscape over time, but they still were able to locate features such as a privy (outdoor toilet) that, when abandoned, was filled with dolls, clay tobacco pipes, a gold pocket watch, and false teeth. They also found the remains of a buried kitchen and a buried doorway into the basement of the Lott House.

Workers in the fields around the Lott House about 1915. Courtesy of Catherine Lott–Divis

The Plymouth Church of the Pilgrims

A photograph of the Plymouth Church, Brooklyn, New York as it looked in about 1904

The Plymouth Church of the Pilgrims was known as the Underground Railroad's Grand Central Depot, named after the famous train station in New York City. This New England–style brick church also had a New England minister, a preacher named Henry Ward Beecher, who became minister there in 1847. Beecher was the brother of Harriet Beecher Stowe, author of the famous 1852 book *Uncle Tom's Cabin*. This antislavery book is given credit for much of the abolitionist movement that sprang up strongly after the 1850 Fugitive Slave Law was passed. Henry Ward Beecher was famous for his fiery sermons against slavery, and every Sunday his church was packed with people—including those who took ferries from Manhattan Island to hear him. So many people came that way that the ferries were called Beecher Boats. One of the riders in 1860 was Abraham Lincoln, who was touring the East for the first time, exploring his chances of winning a presidential election.

Henry Ward Beecher, minister at the Plymouth Church from 1847 to 1877

Some of the slaves who escaped to the North established their own towns or joined other free blacks in settlements. For example, African Americans established Weeksville outside Brooklyn, New York. Census records show that over one-third of Weeksville's inhabitants were born in the South, which probably meant they were escaped slaves. Working at Weeksville after many buildings were torn down, archaeologists found only mixed layers of soil, but they did analyze some artifacts. Similar work is happening at other free black settlements in the North.

The Lott family owned many slaves. They freed their slaves twenty-five years before emancipation was required by New York State. The former slaves were hired back as paid servants. Many of them still worked for the family during the 1840s, when the Underground Railroad movement became so important in Brooklyn.

Secret spaces

The archaeologists did documentary research, map research, and detailed studies of the Lott House. In the house they found two secret rooms.

One was a tiny space hidden in the back of a closet behind some coat hooks. Clothes hung from the hooks would have hidden a doorway in the closet ceiling. When opened, the door revealed three very worn steps leading to another boarded-up door. This door opened into a room in the garret of the house. The room had no windows. It was about 10 feet (3 m) square, and it seemed to have been forgotten over time. Candle wax drippings were found on the floor near the stairs, as though someone had lit the way into this hidden space. While interviewing family descendants, the archaeologists found that two who did not know each other both said that this secret room was where the Lott family kept runaway slaves. The hidden room and the family stories suggest that the Lott House was indeed a stop on the Underground Railroad.

An Underground Railroad room at the Lott House, found while archaeologists were doing "above-ground archaeology." Courtesy of Chris Ricciardi and Alyssa Loorya

An archaeologist uncovers a redware plate at the Lott House. She is brushing off the soil before carefully removing the plate from where it was buried many years ago. Courtesy of Chris Ricciardi and Alyssa Loorya

John P. Parker
HOUSE

Home of freed slave , conductor
on the Underground Railroad,
entrepreneur, foundry owner,
patent holder

National
Historic Landmark

Owned and Operated by the
John P. Parker Historical Society Inc.

For Information
phone 937-392-4188
www.johnparkerhouse.org

Four

An Angel of Mercy

Sometimes, when archaeologists are digging at a site known to be part of the Underground Railroad, they find nothing to confirm this. However, the archaeological results can help explain the kind of person who did the brave work of bringing freedom to African Americans. John P. Parker, a famous conductor on the Underground Railroad, once said, "The real history of this period will never be told . . . for the simple reason that the men who knew dared not tell what they knew."

Archaeologists sift soil through screens during excavations in front of the Parker House steps.

Cast iron gears from the foundry behind the Parker House. Courtesy of Lisa Haitz

Archaeologists' work studied Parker's house in Ripley, Ohio, near Cincinnati. John P. Parker was a former slave. He bought his freedom in 1845 after saving the money he earned working in an Alabama iron foundry (a place where metal is melted and poured into molds to make objects). Parker moved to Cincinnati, Ohio, where he married, started a family, and worked in foundries. From there he relocated to Ripley, where he eventually owned an iron foundry that sat behind his house.

Along with others who lived in Ripley, Parker began rescuing runaway slaves from the South, mostly from Kentucky, sometime in the 1840s. At night, Parker crossed the Ohio River into Kentucky, gathered runaway slaves, and rowed them to safety. His autobiography, as told to a newspaper reporter in the 1880s, contains many exciting tales of his rescue efforts. One time, Parker crept into a plantation house and grabbed a slave baby off the master's bed, where the master was keeping the baby to discourage his slaves from running away. Parker almost was caught that time, but he and the runaway family made it to safety. Some say Parker rescued more than a thousand slaves.

After the Civil War, Parker's foundry burned. He rebuilt his business in a new place, away from his home, and operated it until his death in 1900. Parker was one of few former slaves who held United States patents on two inventions: a machine for breaking up tough sod, and a tobacco press.

Why was archaeology done at Parker's House?

Many changes were needed in order to restore the Parker House. Archaeologists investigated areas that restorers would have to disturb to make sure nothing important would be destroyed.

Digging two test pits next to the house's foundation, excavators quickly found the 1888 fire layer. Large burned timbers, red soils, burned nails, and lots of melted window glass showed that the fire also had damaged the house. Under what probably was a front porch, they found an unusual object: a cast-iron angel. Although very corroded from being buried, the angel had been a delicately cast object, probably made by Parker himself. The angel weighed about 2 pounds (1 kilogram), so it was not something made just for fun. The archaeologists do not know its actual use, but Parker often was called an "angel of mercy," so this certainly is a symbol of his life.

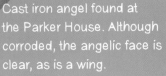

Cast iron angel found at the Parker House. Although corroded, the angelic face is clear, as is a wing.

A ceramic cup from the Parker House, probably broken by the Parkers and now restored by archaeologists. Courtesy of Lisa Haitz

Excavators also uncovered a unique feature in the front yard—a walkway made of cast iron! The iron blocks were about 2 feet (60 cm) square and as much as 3 inches (8 cm) thick. Parker no doubt poured and cast these blocks in his foundry. They showed visitors and passersby how important his business was to him.

The Parkers' six children left buttons, toys such as clay marbles, and a toy vase. The ceramics found at the Parker House are mostly inexpensive kinds, indicating that the family lived simply. Excavations in the iron foundry site behind the house showed that most of it still lies buried in the ground. Uncovered were foundation walls, post holes, wooden floors, the floor of the furnace, and wells. A large, wood-lined box filled with rejected objects still sat near the furnace. A clay floor lay under the entire foundry complex, no doubt to provide a flame-proof surface and to seal off moisture. Studying the evidence of this early foundry will add much to understanding the growth of industry in the United States.

Archaeologists working at the Parker House. Note the river in the background—a nice place to work!

Excavators also found a dog burial. A Labrador-size dog was buried in a pit filled with coal and waste from the furnace. The archaeologists named the dog Clinker, a word that means "used coal."

Why were these finds important?

The archaeological excavations at the Parker House revealed new knowledge about the life of a former slave, as well as information about the workings of a family-owned foundry. Parker was a strong, determined man. He not only purchased his own freedom and then came north to start a new life, but also returned to the South again and again to rescue fellow African Americans. The kinds of artifacts found at his home indicate that he lived simply and probably spent much of his money to help those he rescued. He and his wife raised six children and operated a successful business. He displayed his pride in his work by building an unusual cast-iron walkway in his front yard and by rebuilding his business after fires destroyed it.

The Role of Churches

In addition to the Plymouth Church of the Pilgrims in Brooklyn, hundreds of other churches—especially those with black congregations—became stops on the Underground Railroad. They were located all over the North as well as in the South. The oldest surviving church stop is in Boston. The African Meeting House there has been restored as a museum. Documents reveal that many meetings and dinners were held at the Meeting House, and famous abolitionists like Frederick Douglass spoke there. Archaeological work in the 1980s and again in the 2000s uncovered hundreds of artifacts, such as plates, bowls, platters, cups, knives, forks, and spoons, left from the many meals consumed. Pork, mutton, beef, fish, and duck were some of the meats served. Also found were slate pencils, marbles, and small cups used in the school conducted in the church basement.

Five
Resistance in Kentucky: Fort Nelson

Kentucky stayed in the Union during the Civil War. Lincoln's Emancipation Proclamation freed slaves only in the Confederate states. Thus, slaves in Kentucky did not receive their freedom this way.

A painting done about 1865 shows a Union soldier reading "The Emancipation Proclamation" to slaves and their children.

The Union and Confederate armies fought in Kentucky, each determined to control that territory. The Union army finally won and established Fort Nelson, a large, 4,000-acre (1,620-hectare) camp near Lexington. In 1864 the army issued a proclamation inviting male slaves to join the Union army. If they did, they would be freed—without their owner's permission. Black men flocked to join, and their families—between two hundred and four hundred women and children—went along. Using wood and other materials the army had discarded, the families built a refugee encampment inside Fort Nelson.

The army had not counted on this overwhelming response. The slave owners set up a howl—not only had they lost their male workers, but they had lost the females, too! The women and children were not free—they could not leave!

Black families at Camp Nelson in the new housing area built for them by the Union Army. Courtesy of the Camp Nelson Restoration and Preservation Foundation

But they did. And the army took action. Several times they chased the women and children out of the encampment and dropped them off at least 5 miles (8 kilometers) away. The army threatened to put them in prison if they returned. And once outside the fort, their masters could recapture them. But the families kept coming back. They traveled for miles, carrying children and belongings. They slipped past the army guards at the gates or bribed the guards. How they managed all this is unknown—they had a kind of secret underground railroad of their own.

Finally, the army took decisive action. In November, it burned the encampment to the ground and transported the refugees away on wagons. More than a hundred people died from cold weather or disease.

The news hit the newspapers, and loud protests broke out all over the North. The army reversed its policy and allowed the families to return. In fact, it built a home for them so they did not have to live in shacks. In 1865, an act passed by Congress granted them freedom.

What did the archaeologists find?

No one knew the exact location of the refugee encampment, but they knew it was near a certain warehouse. Archaeologists identified the camp area by heavy ash deposits and many burned artifacts. They found glass, food bone, dishes, dress buttons, coins, a doll head, and beads. One silver half dime was pierced. This is significant because pierced coins intended to be worn have been found at other African-American sites. One former slave said every one of his children wore a half dime around a leg to

Two coins found at the Camp Nelson refugee housing area. One is pierced for wearing, the other is not, but may have been worn inside a shoe for protection against evil spells or bad luck. Courtesy of Stephen McBride

Dogs as Archaeologists

Where was the African-American refugee cemetery at Camp Nelson? The approximate location was known from documents but looking for it using the usual archaeological methods would be very time-consuming and might disturb other features better left undamaged. So they brought in dogs! The dogs sniffed all around and signaled their owners when they smelled something suspicious. For example, eleven-year-old Eagle, a Doberman-mix, would put his head down and his two front paws out until someone stuck a flag in the ground where he indicated a grave would be found. The archaeologists at Camp Nelson have not excavated the area to see if the cemetery actually is located there, but the dogs identified the same area as shown on historic maps. In other projects since this one, however, doubt has been raised as to whether the dogs actually can do this. Eagle's owner admitted burying food bones in at least one archaeology site, so the program has been discontinued.

"Eagle"

fend off witches. The refugees were Christians, but it seems they kept some of their traditional beliefs and customs.

The archaeologists found nails, window glass, and brick in some areas. The presence of glass windows suggests that even in this encampment some people had higher status than others. Some structures had brick or partial brick chimneys. The more expensive ceramics also were found near these dwellings.

The refugees ate mostly wild game. The army was not feeding these people! They must have trapped the game, managed to buy some from the soldiers, or provided labor in exchange for food. Many buttons were found. Some were from officers' uniforms. This suggests that women and children did laundry, using water from the nearby stream, and perhaps did some sewing for pay. Washing clothes for others was something the women could do as a group while watching children play nearby. By setting up their own business, these women would have found a way to be useful and to support themselves.

Why is this discovery important?

The resistance of these women and children to enslavement on a plantation and separation from their husbands is an amazing story. The slave owners could not come onto the military base and recapture them. No matter how many times the army shoved them out, they returned. Again and again. Until the army made a big mistake and took violent action against them.

Archaeologists have discovered the site where this all took place. They have analyzed the artifacts to determine what kind of lives these families led. They have provided the women and children with a "voice" that tells the story of their struggle. They have aroused so much interest in this story that today, 500 acres (200 ha) of Camp Nelson have been set aside by the county, a new museum has been created, and a new highway marker has been installed to tell the story of African Americans at Fort Nelson.

Six

Escape to Canada

Once fugitive slaves crossed the border into Canada, they did not know where to go or what to do. Abolitionists in Canada helped. Many refugees settled in farming communities like Buxton near Lakes Erie and Ontario. Others went into the big cities to find work in mills, stores, and factories.

A monument to the Underground Railroad in Detroit, Michigan. The man and woman are looking toward Canada.

Thornton Blackburn and his wife, Lucie, were two escaped slaves who settled in Toronto, Ontario—but not before they suffered some close calls. In 1831, they crossed the Ohio River from Kentucky to Cincinnati, Ohio. They then settled in Detroit, Michigan. After they spent two years there, a slave agent discovered them and demanded their return. The case went to court, and since they had no certificate of freedom, they were turned over to the sheriff to be returned south. Armed with clubs, stones, and pistols, abolitionists gathered around the jail. The sheriff refused to release the Blackburns. However, he allowed visitors on Sunday. One of the women sat with Lucie Blackburn until dark. The two women then exchanged clothing, and Lucie walked out of the jail. The next day, the sheriff let her friend go free. Abolitionists whisked Lucie across the border into Canada. She was free, but Thornton remained in jail.

The next day, between three hundred and four hundred people rioted outside the jail. When a cart arrived to take Thornton to a steamboat bound

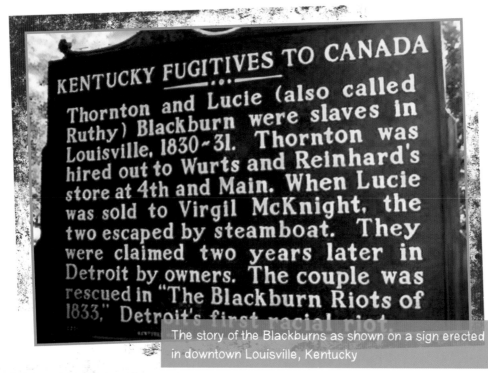

The story of the Blackburns as shown on a sign erected in downtown Louisville, Kentucky

for Kentucky, the rioters seized the horses' heads and pulled the lynchpin from the cart to separate it. When Blackburn appeared at the door, the mob attacked the sheriff. Blackburn was loaded in the cart, the lynchpin was replaced, and the horses galloped away. Once safely in the woods outside Detroit, Blackburn's chains were cut away, and the group ran to the river. However, when they reached Canada, Thornton, his wife, and his helpers were thrown in jail!

Canadian law said slaves who had committed a crime must be returned to the United States for trial. The Blackburns were accused of starting a riot in Detroit. At their trial in Canadian court, Lucie was declared innocent of this, as she was already across the border when the second day's riot occurred. The court decided that Thornton had been in the hands of a man who was acting as a slave agent, not as sheriff. Therefore, since slave agents cannot hold people in jail, Thornton had been held illegally. After five weeks in jail, the Blackburns were released.

Toronto's first "taxicab"

The following year, Thornton and Lucie moved to Toronto. They rented two house lots in an undesirable area on the outskirts of the city. It was covered with forest and dumps created by waste from farms and small industries on the nearby river. According to historical documents, Thornton worked as a waiter in the city. However, he soon saw a need for public transportation. He purchased a horse, had a carriage built, and opened the first cab service in Toronto. His brightly painted red and yellow carriage was a familiar sight around town. By 1848, he was able to buy the land he had been renting. Thornton also became involved with helping other slaves once they got to Canada.

The Blackburns stayed in their original house until Thornton's death in 1890. Lucie then moved to another house they owned after selling the original two lots to the Toronto Board of Education. The board tore down the house and stable, graded (leveled off) the property, and turned it into a schoolyard for the nearby school.

What did archaeologists find at the site?

The Blackburns' site remained buried under the schoolyard. Archaeologists decided to study the site in the 1980s. They found that soil layers associated with the Blackburns' occupation had been disturbed by the grading done

A photograph of the school built near the Blackburns' house. Archaeologists found remains of the former slaves' house and stable in the schoolyard.

when the buildings were torn down. Enough remained to tell the story of their lives, however.

The Blackburns' house and stable were on the same lot. The archaeologists realized that the house was just like a slave family's cabin in the South! The foundation of the house was made of wood laid directly on the subsoil. The outline of the house was revealed by dark stains in the soil caused by the decay of the wood foundation. Apparently, the floors inside the house were wood, as was the roof.

The small, one-story house had a cellar under half of it. A chimney foundation and hearth had stood along the north wall. The chimney had collapsed in domino fashion—the bricks still lay in an overlapping line. The walls and floor of the cellar were both packed dirt. This allowed some water to seep through it. Thornton and Lucie had tried to control this by placing several bricks on the floor against the walls. A large post found off the east wall suggested there once was a porch there.

Apparently, the house inside was divided into two rooms—one for cooking and daily living and one for sleeping. It appears the Blackburns were comfortable here; despite the money they eventually made, they stayed in this house for more than fifty years.

The stable was built later than the house, with its long wall facing the street. It was small with no partitions inside, but documents show that part of it was a story and a half tall. The extra height probably allowed storage of hay for the horse. The earth floor showed burn marks from a wood stove. Thornton probably needed heat while taking care of his cab and horse.

Excavators found evidence of a garden on each lot. Burned garbage, mainly food bone, was uncovered in the yard. Excavators also found evidence that Thornton had burned out tree stumps to clear the property.

Ceramic artifacts found that were used by the Blackburns. The fragment in the upper left is a storage jar. The others are ceramics used for eating and tea drinking.

What do artifacts tell about the Blackburns' lives?

Judging by the artifacts, the Blackburns lived simply and put their money away for retirement. This was a wise move, as they lived for thirty years after Thornton quit his cab business around 1862. The dishes they set on their table were inexpensive, they did not add anything fancy to the original house, and no privy (outdoor toilet) or well was found. The fanciest dishes were tea wares, evidence that they considered each afternoon's teatime an important event. Perhaps they entertained neighbors while pouring tea from their fancy tea set.

Studies of food bone revealed that as in the South, the Blackburns probably preferred to eat mostly pork, followed by sheep and beef. Saw marks on these bones show that the meat came from a butcher shop, although axe marks on some bones suggest that Blackburn chopped up some of the large chunks of meat he brought home from the shop. It seems Blackburn was not very good at chopping. The first marks usually were unsuccessful, so he had to try again and again. The small size and white color of the bones showed they had been boiled. This means Lucie prepared mostly soups and stews.

Wild animal, bird, and fish bones were present, but not in large numbers. These included rabbit, goose, duck, turtle shell, frog, and various fish, all available nearby. Blackburn probably did some recreational hunting and fishing. Chicken bones and eggshells showed they kept domestic birds, too.

The Blackburns had no children, but they kept pet dogs. One found buried on their lot was the size of a spaniel. Gnaw marks made by dog teeth on some of the meat bones in the yard suggests they had a series of such pets.

What have we learned about these escaped slaves?

These two determined refugees found a life for themselves in Canada. Thornton ran a successful business, built a house and stable, and purchased land. The fine tea ware that he and Lucie bought, along with the professionally butchered food they consumed, showed that the couple's wealth increased through the years. The Blackburns lived simply, participated in the abolitionist movement, and prepared for their future. Theirs was a great success story.

Seven

What Archaeologists Found Out

The Underground Railroad Freedom Center opened in Cincinnati in 2004. Visitors are shown viewing an exhibit entitled Escape! during the grand opening.

Although the Underground Railroad was not itself buried in the ground, archaeologists have uncovered evidence of its existence. Slaves resisted their bondage from the very beginning. They even decided to flee south into Spanish territory rather than remain enslaved. Escaped slaves fleeing north found refuge in many different places. Archaeologists have found evidence that they hid in church basements, in the attics of people's homes, and even in underground cisterns.

Many slaves who fled used their skills to create new lives. John Parker started his own foundry. Thornton Blackburn established a successful taxi service. Both men, along with many others, worked on the Underground Railroad to help others achieve freedom. Archaeologists have added much rich detail to the story of the Underground Railroad.

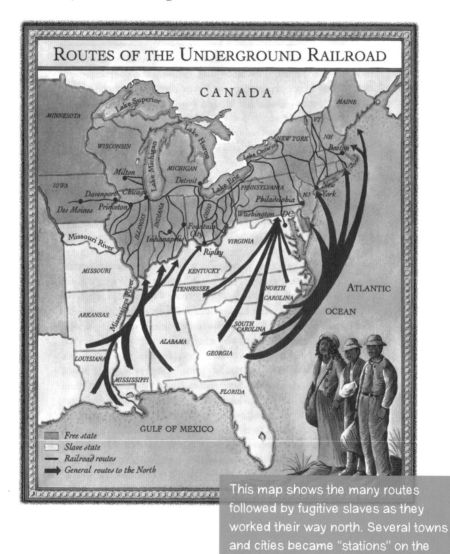

This map shows the many routes followed by fugitive slaves as they worked their way north. Several towns and cities became "stations" on the Underground Railroad.

1619 The first boatload of slaves for sale arrives in Virginia; previously, masters brought their own slaves to North America.

1793 The lieutenant governor of Upper Canada, John Simcoe, helps pass laws to prevent the introduction of slavery in Upper Canada.

1808 Congress prohibits importing more slaves; those already in the United States and their children are still slaves, however.

1827 New York State abolishes slavery.

1829 The governor of Canada welcomes every black man, free or slave, into his land.

1833 The American Anti-Slavery Society is established, linking smaller efforts into a major network.

1834 Slavery is abolished in the British Empire.

1837 Women organize the Anti-Slavery Convention of American Women in New York City as the first women's political convention in the United States. More than two hundred black and white delegates attend, and both blacks and whites become officers.

1838 Frederick Douglass escapes slavery.

1840 Maryland passes a law banning free blacks from traveling in and out of the state.

1849 Harriet Tubman escapes slavery.

1850 The Fugitive Slave Law requires slaves be returned to their masters, even in states where slavery is banned; many flee to Canada.

1851 The Anti-Slavery Society of Canada, headquartered in Toronto, is established.

1857 The United States Supreme Court rules that a slave traveling into a free state is still a slave.

1863 President Lincoln issues the Emancipation Proclamation, freeing slaves in the Confederacy, but not in states that stayed with the Union.

1865 The United States abolishes slavery.

abolition—Putting an end to slavery.

abolitionists—People who wanted to do away with (abolish) slavery.

amendments—Changes to a document, such as the Constitution.

autobiography—A life story told by the person him or herself.

cisterns—Underground structures used to hold rainwater for future use.

confidant—Someone you talk to about your life; a good friend.

conservators—People skilled in the art of saving (conserving) objects such as paintings, furniture, sculptures, textiles, and old documents.

fugitive—Someone running from a place or person.

garret—Room or rooms just below the roof of a house.

militia—A military unit, usually made up of local inhabitants.

passive—Quiet; not resisting.

patents—Documents issued by a government recognizing that an invention belongs to the person who submitted plans and paperwork. This protects the invention from being stolen by others.

refugee—Someone who has left his or her home to escape danger or violence.

strike-a-light—A piece of iron struck against a flint stone to produce a spark for kindling a fire.

Books

Hansen, Joyce, and Gary McGowan. *Freedom Roads: Searching for the Underground Railroad*. Chicago: Cricket Books, 2003.

Larson, Kate Clifford. *Bound for the Promised Land: Harriet Tubman, Portrait of an American Hero*. New York: Ballantine Books, 2004.

Magazine

dig magazine. Entire issue: "Tracking the Underground Railroad," Vol. 5, No. 1, January/February 2003.

Websites

www.archaeology.org/interactivedig

This site features information about many sites under excavation, including the Lott House.

www.hstc.org/frederickdouglass.htm

This site presents a biography of Frederick Douglass and includes several portraits taken during his long career as an abolitionist.

FURTHER INFORMATION

Books and Articles

Armstrong, Douglas V., and LouAnn Wurst. "Clay Faces in an Abolitionist Church: Wesleyan Methodist Church in Syracuse, New York." *Historical Archaeology*, Vol. 36, No. 2, 2003, pp. 19–37.

De Cunzo, Lu Ann, and James H. Jameson Jr., eds. *Unlocking the Past: Celebrating Historical Archaeology in North America.* Gainesville: University Press of Florida, 2005, pp. 38–39.

Deagan, Kathleen, and Darcie MacMahon. *Fort Mose: Colonial America's Black Fortress of Freedom.* Gainesville: University Press of Florida and Florida Museum of Natural History, 1995.

dig Magazine. "Tracking the Underground Railroad," Vol. 5, No. 1, January/ February 2003.

Frost, Karolyn Smardz, *The Thornton Blackburn House and Site.* Archaeological Resource Centre, Department of Continuing Education, Toronto Board of Education, May 1986. Edited by Susan M. Jameison.

————*I've Got A Home in Glory Land: A Lost Tale of the Underground Railroad.* New York: Farrar, Strauss and Giroux, 2007.

Genheimer, Bob. "Underground at the Underground Railroad: Testing at the John P. Parker House and Foundry Site in Ripley, Ohio." Ohio Archaeological Council, Cincinnati Museum Center, 2001.

Harriet Tubman Home. "A Champion of Freedom . . . Harriet Tubman Liberator, Soldier, Missionary." Brochure. Tubman Home, South Street, Auburn, NY 13021, n.d.

Klein, Helen. "Archaeologists Uncover Secret Lott House Rooms." *The Park Slope Courier*, May 2001, p. 21.

McBride, Stephen. "African-American Women, Power, and Freedom in the Contested Landscape of Camp Nelson, Kentucky." Paper presented at Society for Historical Archaeology Conference, Albuquerque, NM, January 2008. Based on a copy of the paper provided by Mr. McBride.

Schuyler, Robert L. *Archaeological Perspectives on Ethnicity in America: Afro-American and Asian American Culture History.* Farmingdale, NY: Baywood Publishing, 1980.

Archaeological excavations at Weeksville and other free black settlements.

Sprague, Stuart Seely, ed. *His Promised Land: The Autobiography of John P. Parker, Former Slave and Conductor on the Underground Railroad.* New York: W. W. Norton & Company, 1996.

Based on notes taken by newspaper reporter Frank Moody Gregg in the 1880s.

Strausbaugh, John. "On the Trail of Brooklyn's Underground Railroad." *New York Times*, October 12, 2007.

Page numbers in **boldface** are illustrations and charts.

About the Author

Lois Miner Huey is a historical archaeologist working for the State of New York. She has published many articles about history and archaeology in kids' magazines as well as a book biography of the Mohawk Indian woman, Molly Brant. She and her archaeologist husband live near Albany, New York, in an old house with four affectionate cats.